AUG - - 2020

Little BLACK PEARLS *for* BLACK GIRLS

Nuggets of Wisdom Every Black Girl (big & small) Should Know

Kennedy
Jordan Turner
THE YOUNG CEO

Kennedy Jordan Turner & Dominique Jordan Turner
Illustrated by Kennedy Jordan Turner

Little BLACK PEARLS for BLACK GIRLS

Nuggets of Wisdom Every Black Girl (big & small) Should Know

Dedication

This book is dedicated to every Black girl around the world. The words and the art are meant to celebrate your beauty, resilience, wit, intellect and magic. Thank you for always carrying the spirit of Harriet, Shirley and Maya. The world needs your spirit now more than ever. We see you.

Keep Shining!

For Daughters

Kennedy shares advice that has helped her to develop confidence and ultimately love the skin she is in! She wants to share these nuggets of wisdom with every little Black girl around the world.

For Moms & Mentors

Dominique thinks that the best gift you can give a young lady is one of self love and confidence. Sometimes us adults need a reminder too! Each pearl of wisdom shared will include a youth and adult perspective so that mom and daughter can read and learn together. Each pearl will include a "Do Together" activity that inspires connection, confidence, love and a deeper appreciation for one another.

1

You are beautiful no matter what shade you come in.

"The kind of beauty I want most is the hard to get kind that comes from within. Strength. Courage. Dignity.

–Ruby Dee

DO TOGETHER

Share with each other the most beautiful quality you admire in the other. Start with the qualities you can't see physically and elaborate on why that quality is important to you.

2

The most important part of your body is your brain.

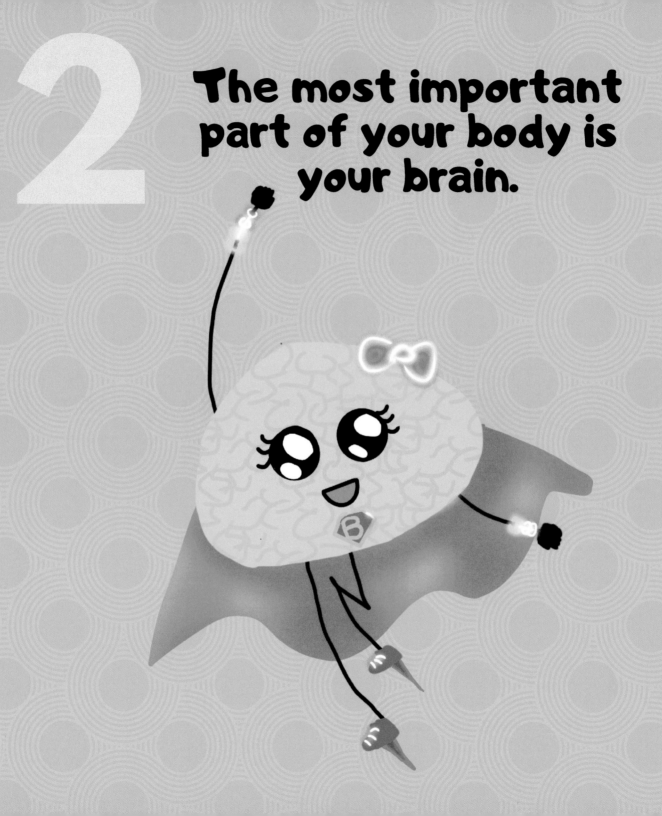

Kennedy
Jordan Turner
THE YOUNG CEO

" We worry so much
about being "pretty"
Let's be:
PRETTY smart
PRETTY kind
PRETTY Strong

DO TOGETHER "

Create a brand new definition for the word "pretty."
What does being pretty mean?
Compare your answers with each other.

3 If you put negative energy into the universe it will come right back to you like a boomerang.

Kennedy
Jordan Turner
THE YOUNG CEO

I know for sure that what we dwell on is who we become.

–Oprah Winfrey

Share three things you are both grateful for. This focus on positivity will create a positive vibration in the universe that will be returned to you just like a boomerang.

4

Even if you are independent, don't be afraid to ask for help.

"

I do my best because I'm counting on you counting on me.

–Maya Angelou

"

DO TOGETHER

Share a story about a time when you needed help. Be open and honest about when you needed extra support and how you went about asking for it.

5

You are going to make mistakes. It won't feel good but it will make you better.

Challenges make you discover things about yourself that you never really knew. They're what make the instrument stretch, what makes you go beyond the norm.

—Cicely Tyson

DO TOGETHER

Think about a challenging time or your "favorite mistake." Talk about a time when you thought it was a mistake but today when you look back at that time, you are glad it happened.

6

There is no such thing as being "too Black" or "not Black enough." God made you perfectly in His image.

Sometimes, I feel discriminated against, but it does not make me angry. It merely astonishes me. How can any deny themselves the pleasure of my company? It's beyond me.

—Zora Neale Hurston

DO TOGETHER

Discuss a quality in the other person that is most like God.

7

Books are your best friend. Reading will take you to places you've never dreamed.

If there's a book you really want to read, but it hasn't been written yet, then you must write it.

-Toni Morrison

DO TOGETHER

Grab five sheets of paper, crayons and markers. You both are going to write a 10 page book together with a story that hasn't been told. Don't think too long about it. Draw pictures, get creative and share ideas.

8

If you're having a bad day, a dance party will cheer you up. Dancing is medicine for the soul.

"

Whatever is bringing you down, get rid of it. Because you'll find that when you're free...your true self comes out.

-Tina Turner

"

DO TOGETHER

Have a mini dance party. Put on Beyonce's song "(Girls) Run the World", turn the volume up, teach each other your favorite dance and then dance like no one is watching!

9 **If you don't see someone who looks like you doing something you want to do, DARE TO BE THE FIRST!**

"

There have been so many people who have said to me, 'You can't do that' but I've had an innate belief that they were wrong. Be unwavering and relentless in your approach.

—Halle Berry

"

DO TOGETHER

Talk about a time when someone doubted you but you did it anyway. How did you feel when they questioned you? How did you feel when you completed the task successfully?

"

You've got to say no to the things that don't honor you. No to the things that don't bring you joy. And you don't have to explain your no.

—Iyanla Vanzant

"

DO TOGETHER

What is something that you want to say "NO" to but you haven't dared to say it? Why do you want to say no?

11 Comparing yourself to other people will only make you sad.

Kennedy Jordan Turner
THE YOUNG CEO

" Embrace what makes you unique. Even if it makes others uncomfortable. I didn't have to become perfect because I've learned throughout my journey that perfection is the enemy of greatness.

–Janelle Monae "

DO TOGETHER

Tell each other what you think makes the other different, unique and special.

12

Choose your friends wisely. They should make you feel good; not bad.

When people show you who they are, believe them the first time.

—Maya Angelou

DO TOGETHER

Talk to each other about your best friend in the world and why you consider them a friend. Then think about someone you used to consider a good friend but no longer has that title. What happened? Discuss desirable characteristics in a friend.

13 Women are leaders. Black girls are leaders. You are a leader. Don't listen to anyone who says anything different.

Kennedy
Jordan Turner
THE YOUNG CEO

"

I thrive on obstacles. If I'm told that it can't be done, then I push harder.

-Issa Rae

"

DO TOGETHER

Grab a pencil, paper and the stopwatch on your phone. Take two full minutes and write down all of the reasons you can think of that make Black women and girls leaders. If your daughter can write, create individual lists and compare them at the end of the two minutes.

14

Be the best you can be. Always do your best.

"

When you've worked hard, and done well, and walked through that doorway of opportunity, you do not slam it shut behind you. You reach back.

–Michelle Obama

"

DO TOGETHER

Think about something you've done that makes you proud. Now think about who helped you achieve that goal. Give them a call to say thank you!

15 Make a great first impression by looking people directly in the eye and shaking their hand firmly.

"

To me, we are the most beautiful creatures in the whole world. Black people. And I mean that in every sense.

—Nina Simone

"

DO TOGETHER

Practice introducing yourself to the other with a strong handshake and direct eye contact. If you truly believe that you are the most beautiful creature in the whole world, looking boldly in someone's eyes won't be a problem.

16

Your hair has SUPERPOWERS. Love and celebrate it.

"

There's not a hair extension or a makeup artist that can make me feel the way I feel when I give back.

-Beverly Johnson

"

DO TOGETHER

Celebrate the beautiful skin you're in by choosing a day to rock your natural beauty. No weave. No make up.
Talk about how it felt.

17

Don't be afraid to be smart. Smart is the new COOL.

Kennedy
Jordan Turner
THE YOUNG CEO

"

I don't know everything. I know a fraction of what there is to know and I don't think I will ever know everything, but it's important to me to constantly challenge myself, to understand different viewpoints, really understand nuance in topics, so I can feel qualified in what I say, so I'm not preaching falsely of what I'm aware of.

-Yara Shahidi

"

DO TOGETHER

Discuss each others "cool factor."
What subject or topic area is a strength?

18

You should have a belly laugh every day. Don't be afraid to be silly.

KENNEDY
Jordan Turner
THE YOUNG CEO

"

Your smile is your logo, your personality is your business card, how you leave others feeling after having an experience with you becomes your trademark.

–Anonymous

"

DO TOGETHER

Tell each other the funniest joke or riddle you know.
If you don't know one, use Google! The cornier the better.
Just laugh!

19

Think highly of yourself. People may say mean things about you. Remember that says more about them than about you.

Confidence Meter

"

If I didn't define myself for myself, I would be crunched into other people's fantasies for me and eaten alive.

-Audre Lorde

"

Discuss your confidence number?
If the Confidence Meter has a scale of 1 to 10 (1=low 10-high) What would need to happen in order for it to grow to a 10?

20

Family is important. Appreciate them.

"

I think that in any family--Black, White, Chinese, Spanish, whatever, family is family. You know that there's dysfunction and that there's this cousin who doesn't like this auntie. But at the end of the day, love brings everybody together.

–Lauren London

"

DO TOGETHER

Have a good laugh about a time when family got together and some of the dysfunction snuck out. How did you react? Have a great big belly laugh about it. It won't be the last time it happens, but it's family!

21 Don't be afraid to love what you love; even if no one else does.

"

If you're doing something outside of dominant culture, there's not an easy place for you. You will have to do it yourself.

-Ava DuVernay

"

DO TOGETHER

Talk about something that each of you want to do that seems unconventional or out of the norm. Commit to supporting each other to achieve that goal. Be each other's biggest cheerleader.

22

Celebrate other girls that look like you. Find something you like about them that you like and share a compliment. It will make her day!

Kennedy
Jordan Turner
THE YOUNG CEO

"

The success of every woman should be the inspiration to another. We should raise each other up. Make sure you're very courageous: Be strong, be extremely kind, and above all be humble.

–Serena Williams

"

DO TOGETHER

Tomorrow when you go to school and work, find two girls/women and identify something you like about them. Share an honest compliment and watch their reaction. At the end of the day, compare notes on the reactions you get.

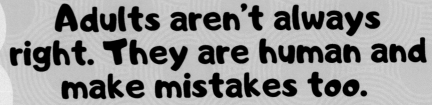

23 Adults aren't always right. They are human and make mistakes too.

Kennedy
Jordan Turner
THE YOUNG CEO

"

Never be limited by other people's limited imaginations.

– Dr. Mae Jamison

"

DO TOGETHER

Ask your daughter about her dreams and share the ones you had when you were her age. The older we get, the more limited we become in our beliefs. We become more practical and impose that pragmatism onto our children. There is so much inspiration that comes from remembering the hopes and dreams we had when we were children.

24

**Be curious.
Ask lots of questions.**

THE YOUNG CEO

"I am a person who believes in asking questions, in not conforming for the sake of conforming. I am deeply dissatisfied — about so many things, about injustice, about the way the world works — and in some ways, my dissatisfaction drives my storytelling.

–Chimamanda Ngozi Adichie

DO TOGETHER

Discuss the most thought provoking question you have ever been asked or would ask someone.

25

Confidence is the most important thing you'll wear each day. It's more important than fancy outfits.

"

It is so liberating to really know what I want, what truly makes me happy, what I will not tolerate. I have learned that it is no one else's job to take care of me but me.

-Beyonce

"

DO TOGETHER

Answer the following questions: Who am I? (You cannot say your name) What truly makes me happy? These seem like elementary questions but can be difficult for most to answer.

26

Never
quit.
ever.

"

If women want any rights more than theys got, why don't they just take them, and not be talking about it.

—Sojourner Truth

"

DO TOGETHER

Imagine the world when your daughter is your age. (Determine the year together) Share what you think life will be like for you both in that year. What is different for Black women? Do you think we will have had a Black woman as President of the United States?

ABOUT KENNEDY

Kennedy is an energetic pre-teen whose confidence is infectious! She is a voracious reader, a passionate dancer, and gifted artist. She is also a fan of coding, science and math. From the time she was born in 2009 she has seen nothing but black excellence. From birth, she has been told that she can be and do anything that she desires, that her skin and hair is beautiful and that her voice and opinions matter. Learn more about Kennedy by visiting www.KennedyJordanTurner.com

ABOUT DOMINIQUE

Dominique is a speaker, leadership coach, CEO and proud mom. She struggled with self-esteem as a child and made it her mission to ensure that her only daughter grew up to know without a doubt that she was more than enough. Today she uses her passion and platform to inspire the next generation of women to become leaders. Dominique has also been recognized for her leadership locally, nationally and globally. One of her proudest accomplishments is being selected as an inaugural Obama Fellow out of 20,000 applicants from over 191 different countries. Learn more about Dominique by visiting www.DominiqueJordanTurner.com

Made in the USA
Monee, IL
23 June 2020